Flippii

PAUL B/

# FLIPPIN' HELL

## DOES THE GOD OF LOVE CONDEMN SINNERS TO EVERLASTING PUNISHMENT?

I have dedicated this book to Ray Lowe. As well as giving me job 20 years ago and being a good friend, it was Ray who encouraged me to give my lecture series on Hell and who gave me strength to come out of the theological closet on the fiery topic of Hell.

## ACKNOWLEDGEMENTS

I guess acknowledgements are really there to say thank you to those who make something possible. Without doubt, therefore, I need to say a huge thank you to the leaders and members of Croydon Jubilee Church for putting up with my ministry for the last 20 years and for giving me the time to pursue the things which God had called me to. You are great church. Thanks to to my wife Ruth who has been my best friend and critic for our 40 years of marriage and has followed me around the world without complaint over that time. Finally I would like to thanks the thousands of Christians who have had a hand in my life, faith and ministry. Bless you all.

# CONTENTS

Acknowledgements

1. The Flippin' Problem    5
2. I Don't Have Presuppositions    16
3. Where The Flippin' Hell Did I Get My Doctrine From?    27
4. Is There Evidence For Flippin' Hell In The Old Testament?    35
5. Flippin' Hell I Haven't Got A New Testament Yet    46
6. Flippin' Hell What Do Jesus And The Apostles Say?    55
7. Flippin' Revelation    66
8. Now I'm Flippin' Confused    76
9. Two Other Flippin' Daft Ideas    80
10. So What The Flippin' Hell Does It Look Like In Hell?    88
11. Flippin' Two faced God    98
12. Flippin' Hell    102

Bibliography    110

## CHAPTER ONE
## THE FLIPPIN' PROBLEM

Breaking News: A British serviceman presumed dead during the first Gulf War in 1991 has been found alive 26 years after being taken captive. He was rescued from a house near Piranshahr in Iran, near the Iraq border.

Intelligence services of British and Iraqi agencies were alerted to the possibility of Sgt Neil Jones' plight three weeks ago. Since then our forces have worked with the cooperation of the Iranian government to locate and liberate the 54 year old Welsh Fusilier. Details of the actual fire fight to free Sgt Jones have not yet been released, but information about his time in captivity is already shocking the world.

It appears that Neil Jones was held in a cellar in complete darkness for nearly all of the nine thousand and four hundred days of his terrible ordeal. He was kept in searingly hot temperatures with only minimal and infrequent issues of food and water, both of which were often infected and caused horrendous dysentery and other diseases. Were this Sgt Jones' only ordeal it would have been terrible enough - separated from family, not knowing what they knew, not seeing his four children grow into adulthood, not knowing if his adored wife had met another man or had even remarried a man who would be the father of his children. Not knowing whether his parents still lived, not even knowing the outcome of the Gulf War or any outside news since his captivity. But the news just coming in from Sgt Jones' debrief is that his 4 captors were deeply sadistic men who, even after they knew of the liberation of Iraq during the *second* Gulf War, continued to torture Neil every day of his imprisonment.

A spokesman for the hospital and debriefing team who are looking after Neil in an undisclosed location has released the following statement today.

"Sgt Neil Jones is in a critical state which is physically comparable to scenes from the liberation of concentration camps at the end of World War Two. We are confident that with modern medicines and nutritional understanding we will be able save his life, although he will not recover his eyesight, or bowel and bladder control. However, our main long term concern is Sgt Jones' mental health. It has become apparent that this man was subjected, on a daily basis, to physical beatings, skin burns with cigarettes, needles pushed under his toe and finger nails and many other kinds of physical and emotional torture too. To say that his treatment has been inhuman would be grossly understating this poor man's plight. He will never be the same again. It is a miracle that he survived as long as he has. The prospects of Sgt Jones ever recovering to anything like a normal life are sadly, nil."

The tabloid headline the next day read:

## "Living Hell for British Soldier"

Thankfully the above story, although based on actual accounts of individuals being held captive in many parts of the world, is entirely made up by me. In fact, although I have grossly exaggerated the time scales here, I could have been very much more graphic in the kinds of things which human beings have done to their fellow men once they have them in their power as prisoners.

Real accounts of people who have been detained against their will and subjected to illegal torture such as the former Archbishop of Canterbury's envoy, Terry Waite or journalist John McCarthy are hard to comprehend, but a common factor in many of these accounts is that, although the physical torture was horrendous, the mental effects were much worse. Not knowing if they would live another day or be executed or subjected to even more inhumane treatment took a huge toll on their mental health.

When I was a Chaplain in the Royal Air Force I spent some time with a young RAF Regiment Officer who had been held hostage during the Bosnia crisis. He told me of the times when his captors held a pistol to his head and pulled the trigger just to see his reaction when he realised that there was no bullets in the weapon. Emotional stresses that will never leave him.

There is no doubt that humanity at its worst can do terrible things to fellow human beings and that those on the receiving end have gone through 'hell'.

In my story Sgt Jones spent a dreadful 26 years in captivity. I'm sure that if his experiences were anything like real life stories, every day would have seemed like an eternity. Perhaps every day he would have hoped that it might come to an end soon. In my story Jones was an innocent recipient of his torture, he had merely done his duty and been unfortunate enough to be captured by the wrong people. In true accounts that is most often the case too. Thankfully, in real life most hostage victims and prisoners of war find their way back, with help, to some form of 'normal' life. For Sgt Jones the period of captivity was stretched so that he broke never to be repaired.

Even though I have read many accounts of former hostages and have met ex POWs, I can't begin to imagine what each day of captivity must have felt like. As I wrote the short story of Sgt Jones, I tried to think what it must have been like to wake up each morning and find I was still in that cell and anticipate what evil might rack my body and mind that day until sleep would give temporary relief (or would it?). Its preposterous to contemplate.

Perhaps this is why few doctrines have troubled human conscience more over the centuries than the traditional view of hell as the place where the lost suffer conscious torment in body and soul for all eternity.

In his book "Love wins" American pastor and writer Rob Bell asks some very searching questions about whether our God would be the kind of captor that we have looked at in my story. Indeed many writers and theologians over the last couple of decades have been asking these questions. Would God, the God who has revealed Himself supremely in Christ Jesus, condemn people of all ages and backgrounds to eternal torture? And lets not pussyfoot around here, we're not talking about the terrible ordeal of John McCarthy which lasted 5 years or my fictitious Sgt Jones' 26 years. We're not even talking about a thousand years, nor a million years, nor even a billion years. We are talking about unending torture for ever and ever, world without end, amen!

Would our God condemn human beings to that?

Could God be even more of a bully and tyrant than the imagined four captors of Sgt Jones?

In fact could God be an unimaginably horrendous torturer?

In the Bible we read that 1 John 4:8 tells us:

> *Anyone who does not love does not know God, because **God is love**.*

Is it ever likely that Christians, people of other faiths and the great undecided are confused when we sport lapel badges or bumper stickers claiming 'God is love!' And then tell them that they will go to hell if they don't confess Jesus as Lord?

What goes through our minds when we sing songs of adoration with lines like Stuart Townend's modern classic:

> *How deep the Father's love for us,*
> *How vast beyond all measure*
> *That He should give His only Son*
> *To make a wretch His treasure*

How do we make sense of Ephesians 3:17-19

## Flippin' Hell

*... so that Christ may dwell in your hearts through faith—that you, being rooted and grounded in love, may have strength to comprehend with all the saints what is the breadth and length and height and depth, and to know the love of Christ that surpasses knowledge, that you may be filled with all the fullness of God.*

It seems to me that we have three different responses possible to our dilemma.

We can do what the Church has tended to do for the last 1,700 years and stay with the hell fire and damnation position which St Augustine formulated. If we do this we have to put up with the huge tension described above that many many people will spend eternity being tortured for their sins committed over three score years and ten. This will also compel us to find an answer for the world that adequately explains what it means that 'God is Love', to define love in a way that explains this position on hell.

Or, secondly, we could abandon the traditional view and adopt a stance, which some have taken in the past and increasingly hold today, which is that "Love" does indeed win and no amount of sin or evil or rejection of Jesus Christ will result in overcoming the almighty force of God's love. So every human being will eventually enter into eternity with God. To do this we would have to redefine and make sense of the huge amount of the biblical passages which speak of hell, judgement, and eternal life.

Thirdly we can try to go back to the time before Augustine, putting aside our presuppositions and ask again 'what do the scriptures actually tell us?' Is there a thoroughly biblical stance which we have perhaps missed?

At the start of my Christian life I took on board the traditional view of hell as a place I really didn't want to risk going to, and I tried to defend it by talking about God's hard love for us, His justice and His defence of His holiness. I learned off pat the answers which I found in tracts and books written by wise evangelical leaders. I even gave these pamphlets to others to help them defend the 'biblical view'.

When I began to train for full time ministry at Westminster College, Cambridge I was immersed in a great deal of teaching by very able scholars and very persuasive writers who drew me towards the second position (often called universalism) whereby God, because of His great love and perfect power will eventually save all mankind. I found that these arguments were incredibly attractive and persuasive. In fact I developed a tic in my right eye as I struggled in real inner turmoil with the thought that I could have not only got it wrong but led others to uphold an unbiblical doctrine on hell. However, I soon realised that, although the case these writers made was extremely attractive, they gave no reasonable answers to the passages on judgement, eternal punishment and hell. In fact they largely ignored those parts of the bible which didn't agree with their point of view. (Something we are all inclined to do). This left me back with the traditional view, now not completely convinced, but with no apparent alternative. Occasionally a theologian would dare to speak about something called 'annihilation' but the idea that some people would just cease to exist seemed a very dodgy one to me. How could it be fair that someone could live their lives denying Christ, even doing overt evil and not be punished in some way. Just dying and that was the end, felt like they were getting off scot free!

So my wonderfully thought through theology on hell, judgement, punishment and eternal life boiled down to the fact that the traditional view must be right because its the one that nearly everyone has nearly always held. The universal view didn't do justice to scripture and the annihilationist view wasn't fair because people got off lightly.

All of this would have been fine if I could settle the arguments put forward on a regular basis from friends who seemed to have a problem that God was a mass torturer on a scale that the world has never known, even when we consider Ghengis Kahn, Hitler, Idi Amin or Pol Pot.

I suppose I would have stayed in my confused state, comforted by my excuse that my view was what the bible taught, had it not been for a tiny seed which fluttered into my mind some years ago when I heard that the brilliant Anglican thinker, John Stott, had become an annihilationist. My initial reaction was, like many evangelicals who heard the news, "Oh no, he's gone over to the liberals!" But the seed had been sown and it was getting well watered by new Christians and those seeking God who kept on asking why would God torture people for eternity. Of course my well rehearsed defence of the Augustinian position convinced many of those who came to me because I'm trained to be able to argue well and after all, as the leader of the church, I must know what is right!

Whether I convinced others with my defence of the traditional doctrine of hell is debatable, but I certainly silenced them into a kind of mutually agreed conspiracy of orthodoxy, whilst sneering at those who dare hold any other, or should I say, heretical position. Oh, by the way, did I mention how I also sneer at those who sanctimoniously hold that they have the truth and everyone else is a liberal lefty?!

## Flippin' Hell

I'm not sure why, but around five years ago I felt that it was time to address the issue of Hell once and for all. I guess I was getting very concerned about some of the books that were coming out which were challenging the traditional view with good questions, but with no real biblical alternatives. So I took six weeks over a summer and read everything I could get my hands on about the doctrine of Hell. I have listed many of these sources in the bibliography to this short book.

Certainly I had got to a point where, on reading yet another pop theology book with a hint of universalism, and fending off yet another question on the fate of the lost I shouted out "Flippin hell, what is the truth?"

## CHAPTER TWO
## I DON'T HAVE PRESUPPOSITIONS

My wife and I love to relax watching box set DVDs of dramas. Usually we hear about them through the recommendation of friends. One of the best of these was when Trevor Payne, the leader of Hope Church Orpington, put us onto "The West Wing" written by the excellent Aaron Sorkin. If you haven't come across the seven series drama based in the West Wing of the White House in Washington, then now is not the time to try to explain the plot. But allow me to indulge my pleasure at the pace of the script with an excerpt from an episode from season two called "Somebody's going to emergency, somebody's going to jail".

The White House Press Secretary, C J Craig and Deputy Chief of Staff, Josh Lyman are in a meeting with members of the Organisation of Cartographers for Social Equality.

```
FALLOW
I'm Dr. John Fallow. This is Dr.
Cynthia Sayles and Professor
Donald Huke.

FALLOW
Plain and simple, we'd like
President Bartlett to aggressively
support legislation that would
```

make it mandatory for every public school in America to teach geography using the Peters Projection Map instead of the traditional Mercator.

JOSH
Give me 200 bucks and it's done.

HUKE
Really?

C.J.
No. Why are we changing maps?

DR. CYNTHIA SAYLES
Because, C.J., the Mercator Projection has fostered European imperialist attitudes for centuries and created an ethnic bias against a Third World.

C.J.
Really?

Fallow brings the map up on the projector.

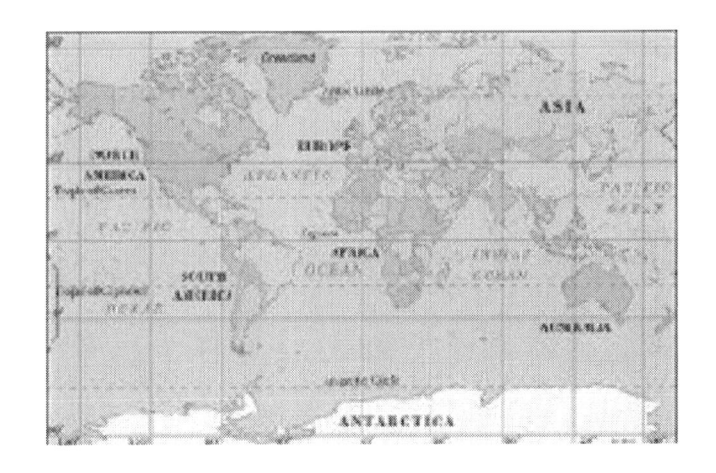

FALLOW
The German cartographer, Mercator, originally designed this map in 1569 as a navigational tool for European sailors.

HUKE
The map enlarges areas at the poles to create straight lines of constant bearing or geographic direction.

CYNTHIA SAYLES
So, it makes it easier to cross an ocean.

FALLOW
But...

## Flippin' Hell

C.J.
Yes?

FALLOW
It distorts the relative size of nations and continents.

C.J.
Are you saying the map is wrong?

FALLOW
Oh, dear, yes.


They go on to point out that despite the appearance on the map, Africa is actually 14 times bigger than Iceland; S America is nearly double the size of Europe; and Mexico is .1 million square miles larger than Alaska. Also countries aren't actually where the map shows them to be. The cartographers then bring up a picture of a map which is made by the Peter's Projection like the one below.

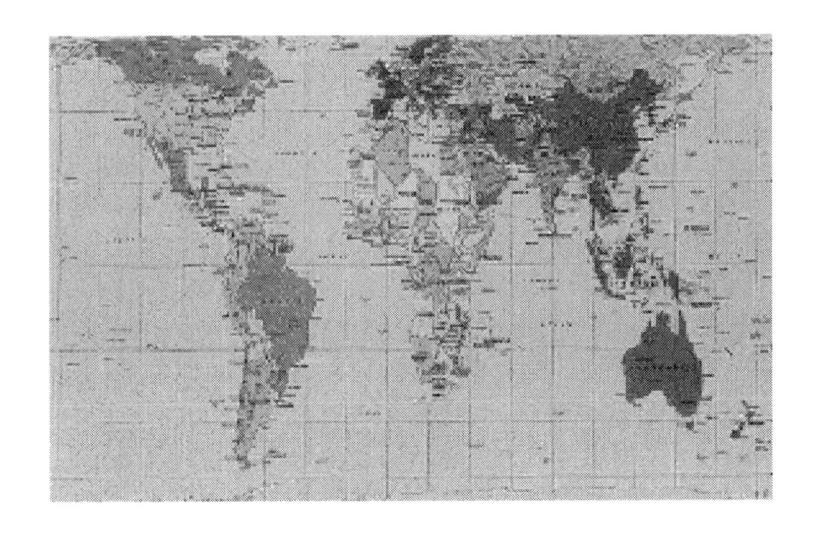

After other scenes have been played out in the episode the cameras return to the briefing room

Cartographer 1
Salvatore Natoli of the National Council for Social Studies argues "In our society we unconsciously equate size with importance, and even power".

Cartographer 2
When Third World countries are misrepresented they're likely to be valued less. When Mercator maps exaggerate the importance of Western civilisation, when the top of the map is given to the northern hemisphere and the bottom

## Flippin' Hell

is given to the southern... then
people will tend to adopt top and
bottom attitudes.

C.J.
But... wait. How... Where else
could you put the Northern
Hemisphere but on the top?

SAYLES
On the bottom.

C.J.
How?

FALLOW
Like this.

The map is flipped over.

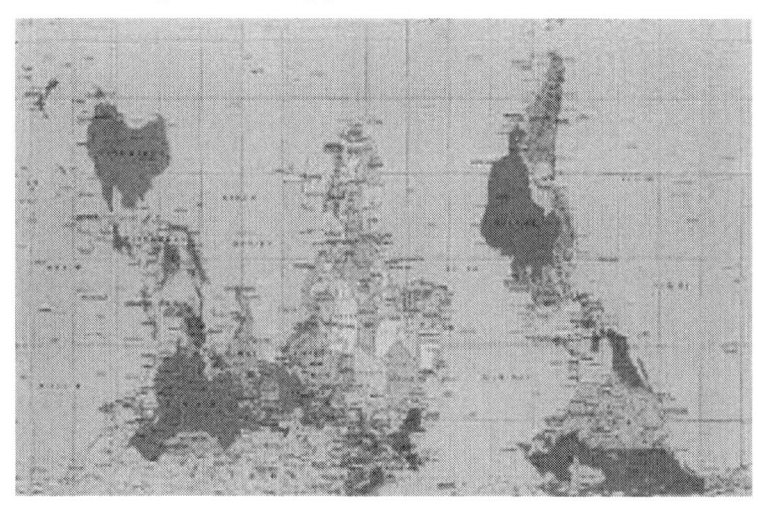

C.J.
Yeah, but you can't do that.

FALLOW
Why not?

C.J.
'Cause it's freaking me out.


Well the scene from that episode was meant as a light relief from the main plot but whether the Cartographers for Social Equality exists or not, it may surprise you to know that the points made are true.

Everyone of us has grown up with school atlases that have given us a presupposition of what the world looks like. Of course we know that its actually a sphere (Well its actually not a sphere but an oblate spheroid, but hey!) but our maps have misrepresented sizes and places quite a lot. And as the fictional Fallow says in the episode "who says it should be so?".

In fact we could go further than the West Wing writers and look at it, not from just Peters projection or just upside down, but even who put the middle in the middle. Australian map makers might suggest the following:

## Flippin' Hell

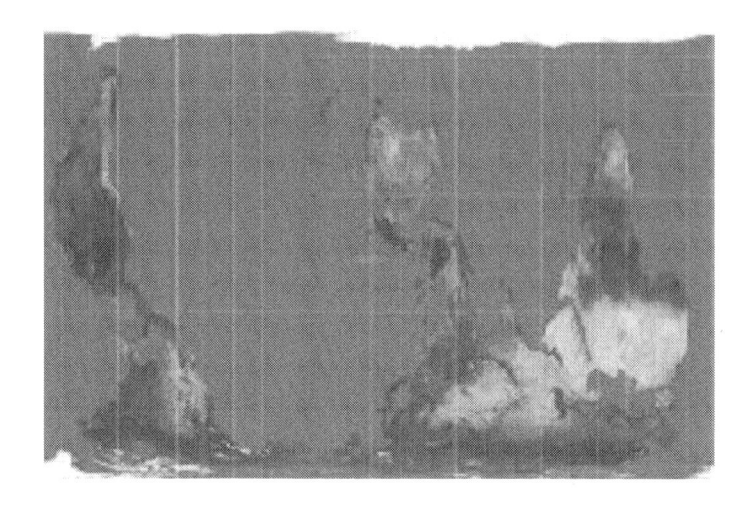

By now you are probably wondering why you ever began to read this book. You certainly didn't expect to be educated in the ways of the West Wing or nuances of cartography. I expect that you want to know what the 'flippin hell' I'm saying about flippin' hell.

My point is that we can have the right heart about something and be utterly sincere in our beliefs, but be utterly wrong because of our presuppositions.

Maybe you think that the way you see the world doesn't have much of an impact on your every day life. However, it may well affect the decisions you make over the course of your life, even how you relate to those living around you who originate from other countries, faiths, or cultures.

One of the things about our presuppositions is that we, like CJ in the sketch, aren't really aware of them until they are challenged. They are like sets of lenses that sit in front of our eyes through which we look at the world around us. Rather like those who have had operations to remove cataracts who often report that they had got so used to seeing the world in a hazy, colourless ways, that they were shocked at how vivid the world looked upon recovery from their operation.

A few years ago I delivered 6 hours of lectures in one day to a group of church leaders on the subject of hell (It probably seemed like hell to those attending). One pastor struggled with the idea of challenging his fairly traditional view of hell, even though he too did not like the idea of eternal punishment for the lost. A couple of months later he told me that during his morning bible readings he had particularly looked at the passages on judgement and hell and was shocked that some of the ways he had read some scriptures were now changed because they didn't necessarily read the way in which he had always thought.

In fact you can do a little test of your own here. We don't have to go to complicated reading of obscure greek verbs. Just think about the way

## Flippin' Hell

you read an email or a text from a friend. You will read it with a presupposition as to how that friend feels about you or the particular subject matter.

For instance, if you and I fell out one evening and the next day I sent you a text saying "Please meet me at the cafe at 11am to apologise" I might mean I want to apologise but you may read it that I expect you to. The tone of voice you hear in your head could completely change the meaning.

I have fallen foul of this type of presupposition on numerous occasions. I usually then spend time working out what I'm going to say and what the other person will reply and so on, through a whole conversation which ends in me resigning my job or starting world war three before I've even spoken to that person!

Just over a century ago it would have been very difficult to say the things we are looking at over the next few chapters. The collective presuppositions of the churches were such that to question any of them would result in excommunication, being ostracised or losing your lively hood or even losing your life. We have only to look back at the reformation when protestants disagreed with catholics, as to the violence each party inflicted on the other!

Sociologists tell us that we live in a post modern era. One of the distinctives of this is that post modern people, ie those under 40 today, tend to easily question presuppositions and absolutes which we held as unquestionable. Whilst I am not a fan of where post modernism tries to take us, I really like the fact that we are now living in a time when we can question presuppositions without burning one another at the stake. We can admit that we may have got it wrong even though our heart has been right.

I really hope that if you, like me, are over 40 you will stay with me through the next chapters as I try to take off the lenses I grew up with and honestly deal with what the Bible actually says about hell. If you are under 40 I hope that you enjoy the dismantling of some of the prepositions that have been around for centuries.

## CHAPTER THREE
## WHERE THE FLIPPIN' HELL DID I GET MY DOCTRINE FROM?

The 20th century philosopher Bertrand Russell blamed Jesus for teaching a doctrine of hellfire and for the untold cruelty that such a doctrine has caused in Christian history.

Can that be the case? If so Jesus would be worse than the cruel torturers of Sgt Jones.

Well the early church was divided on this doctrine. As we have already seen, in the 5th century Augustine defined the view largely now held. But in the 3rd century Irenaeus, who was the Bishop of what we now know as Lyon in France, held the view that those not in Christ would face annihilation. This was no isolated opinion. In fact Irenaeus was a disciple of a guy who was a disciple of the Apostle John! Trump that one!!

Later on in the 4th century Pope Gregory believed that all would eventually be saved, much like modern universalists.

Why did these men have such different views? The answer is just the same as today, their presuppositions.

Actually, to decide on a doctrine of hell is too large a subject to tackle in one bite. There are several parts to the argument that need to be built up.

It would be like building a new home by saying to a builder 'build me a house'. I could end up with something I really didn't want or need. To get the house I want I would have to say how many rooms, where, what size, what shape, what price, how many windows etc

Some of the building blocks to this debate are usually:

1. Are we naturally immortal or does salvation grant us eternal life?
2. How can we have a free will and yet God be sovereign? Can both be true?
3. Can we be saved after we die?
4. What does God do about those who refuse Him?
5. What does the Bible say about punishment?
6. What does the Bible say about judgement?
7. What does the Bible say about eternity?

When we build a house the first thing we need is a foundation, otherwise the whole thing will come tumbling down. The foundation for our doctrine of hell must be found in the New Testament. But that must also be dug out of our understanding of what the Old Testament tells us, and the literature written between the end of the Old and the beginning of the New Testaments.

One of the subjects students at bible colleges learn is called 'hermeneutics', it's the process of interpreting the scriptures. At college I learned about three basic principles when interpreting what the Bible says. Our tutors told us:

1. Always study the clear obvious passages before looking at the difficult or obscure ones. Then interpret difficult passages in the light of the clear ones.

2. Always study literal passages before looking at figurative ones. Figurative passages should be interpreted within the doctrinal boundaries set by the literal passages.

3. General truths should be grasped before looking at details.

C S Lewis wrote a lovely essay which touched on this called 'Fern-seeds and Elephants". The main point of the essay was that scholars can spend all of their time looking in scripture for tiny things and miss the big, clear, obvious point.

One of our problems today is that we rarely take time to look at any doctrine in this way, in fact we haven't been taught to. We have been given the preacher's answer to our questions which goes something like this:

"I have studied this doctrine and this is the answer so now you need to believe the answer and I will teach you how to defend it as I have just done". There wouldn't be too much of a problem with this if the teacher had actually done the study, but I have found that that is not often the case.

What happens with most teaching is that we start with the accepted belief and then learn how to defend that belief to others.

Let me show you what I mean.

I have taught my children that West Bromwich Albion are actually the best football club in England. How do I know that, well thats what my friends and family told me and that is how I was raised. I can defend that by telling you that my dad told me we won the FA cup 5 times. We began in 1878 and were founder members of the football league in 1888 when we won the FA Cup for the first time. In 1954/5 we were the first team to win the League Cup and FA Cup in the same season.

All of the above details are true and to a born and bred Albion fan (come on you Baggies) West Brom are the best in the world. Now there are those in my office who disagree with me. However, they don't counter my arguments with their team's history but with plain facts about recent results. Fools every one of them.

When I indoctrinated my kids to the ways of the Baggies, I didn't give them the facts, I gave them stories to support my predisposed position. They in turn accepted the 'facts' that their infallible father fed them and hopefully will continue to one day support the Albion and raise their children in a similar way. Sadly my oldest daughter is already backsliding as she married a Leicester City fan.

Let me say that I respect bible colleges for what they teach today, but I am dismayed that I rarely hear of any course where a student for ministry is encouraged to do really good in depth study of any doctrine. Most preachers in most pulpits on most Sundays have merely learned to defend the status quo (so whatever you want goes rocking all over the world.. pause for tumbleweed). Therefore life long Christians in their churches have similarly learned from their teachers and some of them have gone on to teach and preach and so on and so on.

Could it possibly be that we have developed more of our doctrine on hell from our past than from the New Testament?

With few exceptions, the traditional view of hell has dominated Christian thinking from the time of Augustine to 20c.

Let me remind you again that this view states that immediately after death the souls of the lost descend into hell, where they suffer the punishment of a literal eternal fire. At the resurrection, the body is reunited with the soul, so the pain of hell intensifies for the lost and the pleasure of heaven for the saved.

**So why the flippin hell do we still hold to this view?**

We owe so much of our understanding of hell to the middle ages, often called the dark ages!

Some creative medieval minds have pictured hell as a bizarre horror chamber where punishment is based on an eye for and eye principle. William Crockett in his book '4 views on Hell' says:

*"In Christian literature we find blasphemers hanging by their tongues. Adulterous women who plaited their hair to entice men dangle over boiling mire by their neck or hair. Slanderers chew their tongues, hot irons burn their eyes."*

These early images of hell were immortalised by the 14c Italian poet, Dante Alighieri. In his

## Flippin' Hell

*'Divine Comedy'*, he writes of hell as a place of complete terror, where the lost writhe and scream while the saints enjoy the glory of paradise above.

At the reformation in the 16th century Luther and Calvin were more reserved than their predecessors, but others that followed them seemed to feed off the medieval view.

In 18th century the great American evangelist Jonathan Edwards pictured hell as a raging furnace of liquid fire that fills both the body and the soul of the wicked:

*"The body will be full of torment as full as it can hold, and every part of it shall be full of torment. They shall be in extreme pain, every joint of them, every nerve shall be full of inexpressible torment."*

In 19th century the Baptist preacher Charles Surgeon said:

*"In fire exactly like that which we have on earth thy body will lie, asbestos-like, forever unconsumed, all thy veins roads for the feet of Pain to travel on, every nerve a string on which the Devil shall for ever play his diabolical tune of hell's unutterable lament."*

Its not difficult to see where we received our views from. The question is not, 'can we defend the traditional view with biblical texts', it is 'Is the traditional view true'.

In other words, if we were to formulate a doctrine of hell from scratch with no prior knowledge of the Augustinian view, what would we find?

## CHAPTER FOUR
## IS THERE EVIDENCE FOR FLIPPIN' HELL IN THE OLD TESTAMENT?

I remember hearing the sixties singer Helen Shapiro giving her testimony at a concert about 18 years ago. She had become a Christian from a Jewish upbringing and, prior to her conversion, had been pursued by a Christian who kept showing her the Bible. Then one day someone pointed out that the names of people in the New Testament were Greek forms of their original Jewish names. Even 'Jesus' was 'Joshua'. Miss Shapiro told the story of wanting to check this out by reading the Jewish Bible so she went into a Jewish bookshop in London and asked the man behind the counter for an Old Testament. He replied "How *old* would you like it to be?"

The point of the story, of course, is that for the Jews there is no Old Testament its just the Bible. They don't recognise the New Testament. But a further point is that the Jewish Bible and our Old Testament are different in one obvious way. The Tanakh (Jewish Bible) has its books in a very different order after Judges:

| Tanakh | Old Testament |
|---|---|
| 1 +2 Sam | Ruth |
| 1+2 Kings | 1+2 Samuel |
| Isaiah | 1+2 Kings |
| Jeremiah | 1+2 Chronicles |
| Ezekiel | Ezra |
| Hosea | Nehemiah |
| Joel | Esther |
| Amos | Job |
| Obadiah | Psalms |
| Jonah | Proverbs |
| Micah | Ecclesiastes |

The lists continue in their different orders. What I found when I read the Hebrew Bible was that the order changed how I understood certain things.

Following on from my discovery I realised that neither of the orders in which the Tanakh and Old Testament are arranged are actually the chronological order of the events covered by the books. And most importantly of all, the books are not arranged in order of when they were first written either.

If we put the books in order of when they were first written many scholars would list them:

Leviticus
Job
Exodus
Deuteronomy
Genesis
Numbers
Joshua
Judges
Ruth
Song of Solomon
Ecclesiastes
1+2 Samuel
Psalms
Proverbs
Jonah
Amos
Joel
Hosea

Of course, we'll probably never know the true order of when the books were written but my point is that when we try to get them close to the correct order, its possible to read the development of thoughts of the Hebrews as they grow in their understanding of God and as they receive His continuing revelation.

In the parts of the Old Testament written quite early, its clear that there was no expectation of a man living for ever after the fall in Genesis 3.

Ie **Gen 6:3** Then the LORD said,

*"My Spirit shall not abide in man forever, for he is flesh: his days shall be 120 years."*

Death was simply the end of life. ie 1 Sam 28:3

*'Now Samuel had died, and all Israel had mourned for him and buried him in Ramah, his own city.'*

He died, full stop. So death was an event not a state.

The place of the dead had a word – 'Sheol'.

In earliest writings we can find three things about Sheol:

- a. with the exception of Num 16:33 Sheol was never used to describe the event of death.
- b. Sheol was the place that both the righteous and wicked went
- c. It was just under the earth somewhere and no one returned from there. It was linked with burial and was therefore seen as a dark and silent place.

So, when I looked at the earliest books of the Old Testament I found that death was just the end of life. Full Stop.

"But" I hear you say, "enough of this clever clogs stuff, what about Genesis 2 and 3?"

Of course its in these chapters that we learn so much from God about the purposes of man and our relationship with God.

One of the building blocks I said we would need would be to resolve the issue of whether mankind has eternal life in our own right or whether we are merely mortals who will die without God's intervention. What does Genesis 2 and 3 tells us about this, did the fall change anything?

Lets look at Genesis 2:17, 3:19, 3:22f

> **Gen 2:17** *"but of the tree of the knowledge of good and evil you shall not eat, for in the day that you eat of it you shall surely die."*

Both Adam and Eve ate the fruit but neither keeled over and died so it must be a metaphoric message or their death was delayed until much later. Either way, without sin, man may have been immortal, though neither option gives us any reason to believe that man was so after the fall.

***Gen 3:19*** *"By the sweat of your face you shall eat bread, till you return to the ground, for out of it you were taken; for you are dust, and to dust you shall return."*

The curse here will remain in effect until death. So its very clear that humanity was definitely mortal after the fall.

***Gen 3:22*** *Then the LORD God said, "Behold, the man has become like one of us in knowing good and evil. Now, lest he reach out his hand and take also of the tree of life and eat, and live forever—"*

This verse seems to imply that mankind might have expected to live forever before the fall, but certainly not afterwards.

Its reasonable to see that the earliest writings of the Bible show us that without any intervention of God, as in Enoch for example, fallen man lived, and died and that was that.

### Life and death in later Old Testament

Sheol is mentioned much more in later Old Testament. Its still a place of the dead but now in 8 verses, (Psalms 9:17, 16:10, 49:15f, Proverbs 5:5, 7:27, 9:18, 15:24, 23:14) it's begun to be seen as 'a place of condemnation', but there's no mention of a corresponding place of reward like heaven.

Its not until we start to read the much later parts of the Old Testament that we find ideas of eternal punishment. As in Isaiah 66:22-24 and Daniel 12:1-2.

## Isaiah 66:22-24 The Fate of the Wicked.

*"For as the new heavens and the new earth that I make shall remain before me, says the LORD, so shall your offspring and your name remain. From new moon to new moon, and from Sabbath to Sabbath, all flesh shall come to worship before me, declares the LORD. "And they shall go out and look on the dead bodies of the men who have rebelled against me. For their worm shall not die, their fire shall not be quenched, and they shall be an abhorrence to all flesh."*

When I was trying very hard to believe the traditional view of hell, I used this passage as a proof of eternal punishment.

But should we read it that way?

The setting of the passage is the contrast between God's judgment upon the wicked who will be punished by "fire" and His blessings upon the righteous who will enjoy prosperity and peace, and will worship God regularly from Sabbath to Sabbath.

Isaiah's description of the fate of the wicked was possibly inspired by the report of the Lord's slaying of 185,000 men of the Assyrian army during the reign of Hezekiah. We're told that "when men arose early in the morning, behold, these were all dead bodies" (Is 37:36). "Worms" are mentioned because thats what people were used to seeing with dead bodies, because they are part of decomposition and represent the horror of corpses left to rot in the open.

'Fire that shall not be quenched' is used frequently in Scripture to signify a fire that consumes (Ezek 20:47f) and reduces to nothing (Amos 5:5f; Matthew 3:12).

Another of the box DVD series that Ruth and I love to watch is the American drama 'Bones' which follows the adventures of an FBI agent and his partner who is a forensic anthropologist. A common theme over the 8 series that we have watched so far (Yes I am that sad) is bodies that get found which have either been buried and are covered with maggots or burned. The DVDs are rated 15 because the scenes are gruesome to say the least.

To any generation, worms and fire are vile symbols of death and destruction.

In our passage from Isaiah the image of an unquenchable fire is simply designed to convey the thought of being completely burned up or consumed. Its got nothing to do with everlasting punishment of immortal souls. It's clearly dealing with dead bodies which are consumed.

## Dan 12:1f "Everlasting Contempt"

*At that time shall arise Michael, the great prince who has charge of your people. And there shall be a time of trouble, such as never has been since there was a nation till that time. But at that time your people shall be delivered, everyone whose name shall be found written in the book. And many of those who sleep in the dust of the earth shall awake, some to everlasting life, and some to shame and everlasting contempt.*

The second Old Testament text I used to support the 'hell as everlasting punishment theory' was Dan 12:2, which speaks of the resurrection of both good and evil.

When I spent the summer reading up on hell I found that many scholars looked closely at the last word of verse 2, the Hebrew word "deraon" translated "contempt" which also appears in Isa 66:24 where its translated "abhorrence"

In his commentary on *The Book of Daniel,* André Lacocque says that the meaning of deraon in Dan 12:2 and in Isa 66:24 is the decomposition of the wicked.

It seems that the contempt is caused by the disgust over the decomposition of the bodies, and not by the never-ending suffering of the wicked.

I began to realise that, very much to my surprise, the Old Testament evidence for the everlasting punishment of the wicked is negligible, if not non-existent.

But verses which show the total destruction of the lost are all over the place if we care to look through new lenses. The lost will:

perish like the chaff (Ps 1:4, 6),
be dashed to pieces like pottery (Ps 2:9, 12),
be slain by the Lord's breath (Is 11:4),
be burnt in the fire "like thorns cut down" (Is 33:12),
die like gnats (Is 51:6).

Perhaps the clearest description of the total destruction of the wicked is found on the last page of the Old Testament:

## Flippin' Hell

*For behold, the day is coming, burning like an oven, when all the arrogant and all evildoers will be stubble. The day that is coming shall set them ablaze, says the LORD of hosts, so that it will leave them neither root nor branch.*
*Malachi 4:1*

The image of the all-consuming fire which leaves "neither root nor branch" suggests utter consumption and destruction, not perpetual torment.

# CHAPTER FIVE
# FLIPPIN' HELL, I HAVEN'T GOT A NEW TESTAMENT YET

To try to understand what the New Testament teaches us on the subject of hell and eternal life we need to know what the people we find in the New Testament thought. What were their presuppositions. Clearly they got their understanding from the Old Testament and from what they had received in the period following the end of their scriptures until the coming of Christ, in as far as God had revealed it to them and world thought had convinced them.

The New Testament doesn't often help us with these presuppositions, even though the original hearers understood what their own world view was, its hard for us to. Although I did have a chat with Dr Who and he said .... 'ah no, sorry that was a dream I had last night'.

Like today, the people in AD40 held widely differing views on human destiny. So there's plenty of scope for appealing to the wrong presuppositions, ie. ones that weren't believed by the apostles.

What did Jesus and the New Testament writers mean by terms like 'Gehenna', 'the world to come', 'the resurrection', and 'reward'? All these terms were largely foreign to the Old

Testament and they are not really defined in the New Testament.

When I came to do my reading on Hell in the New Testament I tried hard to study the epistles and gospels in the light of its own presuppositions rather than my 21st century ones. Jesus used the language and thought forms of his day. His day was 200 years after the last Old Testament thinking! What happened in those 200 years is of immense importance if we are to try to understand what was in the minds of first century Jews.

So lets have a little look at what happened between the close of the Old Testament and the birth of Jesus.

We know that the Jews had been in exile in Babylon and then came back to rebuild their nation. When the people returned from exile in 500s BC, they expected God to vindicate them and give them a new city, and temple etc.

Clearly things weren't quite what they expected. The Zerubbabel temple wasn't a patch on Solomon's and Israel's less than helpful neighbours continued to oppress them.

In 332BC the Jews were no match for Alexander the Great's General Parmenio who made quick work of occupying the land and subduing the people. After that the province ping ponged between Egyptian and Syrian rulers for 100 years, finally to be completely subsumed in the Greek empire. The Greek language and culture began to take more and more hold of the people and therefore changed their hopes and expectations.

At the end of the year 167BC, by order of Antiochus IV Epiphanes, King of Syria and therefore the then ruler of the Jews, the Temple of Zion was desecrated and given over to idolatry and the law of Moses was declared null and void. Anyone found observing the commandments of the Torah was tried and executed and the Jews were forced to worship the gentile's gods, even to offer them pigs which were considered unclean to good Jews. This led some Jews to believe that they were in the times the prophets foretold, the last trial, the Day of the Lord.

The Jewish people had had just about enough of long term oppression and so came about the Maccabean revolt.

In the narrative of I Maccabees, after Antiochus issued his decrees forbidding Jewish religious practice, a rural Jewish priest from Modiin, Mattathias the Hasmonean, sparked the revolt against the Seleucid Empire by refusing to worship the Greek gods. Mattathias killed a Hellenistic Jew who stepped forward to offer a sacrifice to an idol in Mattathias' place. He and his five sons fled to the wilderness of Judah. After Mattathias' death about one year later in 166 BC, his son Judah Maccabee led an army of Jewish dissidents to victory over the Seleucid dynasty in guerrilla warfare, which at first was directed against Hellenized Jews, of whom there were many. The Maccabees destroyed pagan altars in the villages and circumcised boys.

The revolt itself involved many battles, in which the light, quick and mobile Maccabean forces gained notoriety among the slow and bulky Seleucid army, and also for their use of guerrilla tactics. After the victory, the Maccabees entered Jerusalem in triumph and ritually cleansed the Temple, reestablishing traditional Jewish worship there and installing Jonathan Maccabee as high priest. A large Seleucid army was sent to quash the revolt, but returned to Syria on the death of Antiochus IV. Its commander Lysias, preoccupied with internal Seleucid affairs, agreed to a political compromise that restored religious freedom.

What started as a Maccabean revolt ended up as the Hasmonean dynasty, which in turn proved to be just as unjust as the Syrians had been.

If we had gone back to 170BC in the TARDIS we would have probably seen the Jews welcoming the revolt, believing that at last God was establishing His Holy state centred on Jerusalem. But it wasn't to be, and within 100 years Jerusalem and the whole nation had fallen to the next occupiers, the Romans.

Until this point many Jews thought that salvation would come for the nation of Israel in this life through the establishment of God's people ruling their own land in perfect harmony with His messiah at the head. But now, in some of the writings of the day, we begin to see another trend in a belief in an everlasting punishment for the wicked after death and for the righteous to have everlasting life.

## Roman Rule and its affects on thinking

Just as the Greek influence changed the Jewish thoughts and lifestyles, now just before the birth of Christ the Romans ruled Palestine and their thoughts were being intermingled with those that had gone before.

Largely the Jews complied with the new powers, but different sects reacted differently. In particular the Sadducees and the Pharisees. The Sadducees did very well under their new masters and so kept the status quo at all costs. They denied God's intervention, or any kind of after life. They were really materialists, what mattered was what you did now.

The Pharisees were more popular. They were particularly concerned with questions of righteousness because they believed that the Messiah would return if Israel cleaned up her act. As self proclaimed experts in legal interpretation, the Pharisees held that a man's soul was immortal and therefore they expected punishment and reward after death including resurrection for good people and eternal punishment for the souls of others. In 'The Testament of Moses', written at roughly the time of Jesus, its shown that they held a belief that the righteous Jews will gain a celestial existence whilst the gentiles will be destroyed. Another book from the time of Jesus 'Pseudo Philo' speaks about the hope that God would visit the earth, raise the dead, put an end to death and establish a new heaven and earth. The wicked would be judged. 'Hell' was thought of as a place of all the dead prior to resurrection which ceases to function on the day of judgement

## The Targum

We can't be sure which or how the many of the writings from the time of Jesus influenced the thoughts of early first century Jews, but the works that we do know were of great influence were the Targum and other writings of the Rabbis of the time. The Targums were largely versions of Old Testament books written in

Aramaic rather than Hebrew or its Greek translation.

Without doubt Jesus and the Jews of his time would have been very familiar with the writings in the Targum. So the language and understanding of the New Testament writers, although inspired by the Holy Spirit would have drawn on thoughts from the Targum. Four particular phrases in the Targum have been particularly useful in my study of hell, "The world to come", "Reward and punishment", "Gehenna"/"Gan Eden", and "Judgement".

## The World to Come

In the Targum "The world to come" is used as "another place' entered into after death, rather than "another time". At death Jews all immediately went there. So it wasn't due to God's action it was natural immortality.

## Reward and Punishment

Punishment in the Old Testament is rarely an end in itself. But in the Targum it's quite different. In the world to come an individual's sins are punished. Again, "Reward" wasn't common in Jewish thought, but in the Targum all actions in this life had punishment or reward in the life to come.

## Gehenna/Gan Eden

Because there would be punishment and reward in the world to come, this world acquired a name. Gan Eden became the name for the place of the righteous and Gehenna for the world of the wicked. The Targum sated that at creation first God created the Law, then Gehenna and Gan Eden.

'Gehenna' isn't found in the Hebrew Bible, our Old Testament, only in the Targum in Aramaic and 3 other non biblical writings of the time of Jesus. It's the place where punishment comes in the world to come but also for the punishment itself. Sometimes it's a place of fiery punishment sometimes annihilation. The wicked were in Gehenna and no further explanation was needed it was such a terrible fate.

## Judgment

Here the Targum is very clear. The time of judgement is at the point of the individuals death and precedes reward or punishment and so the gateway to Gehenna or Gan Eden.

The great Rabbis of this time, Shammai and Hillel (Both Pharisees) disputed the nature of Gehenna and came up with differing durations spent there. Both Rabbis agreed that the righteous went straight to eternal bliss and the wicked to Gehenna, but Rabbi Hillel taught that those who were neither righteous or wicked would go to Gehenna for one year and then be annihilated.

One thing that all literature seemed to agree on was that Gehenna was to be avoided at all costs.

It would seem that there was no consistent "Jewish view" of the fate of the wicked at the time of Jesus, though most of the documents reflect the Old Testament view of the total extinction of sinners, some clearly speak of the unending torment of the wicked.

Our question is still 'what did Jesus believe?'.

## CHAPTER SIX
## FLIPPIN' HELL, WHAT DO JESUS AND THE APOSTLES SAY?

### Did Jesus Teach Eternal Torment?

Surely if Hell is a place of eternal torment then the best proof will be found in what Jesus said. Indeed, many contemporary writers believe in the traditional view of eternal torment because they have found that it is exactly what Jesus taught. The great Australian theologian, Leon Morris wrote:

*"Why does anyone believe in hell in these enlightened days? Because Jesus plainly taught its existence."*

But is this true? We must not begin to form a doctrine on Hell of any sort until we are very sure about what Jesus actually said.

In fact, Jesus uses the term *Gehenna* (translated "hell" in our Bibles) 7 out of the 8 times the word occurs in the New Testament. The other reference is found in James 3:6.

So already we can say that the issue isn't 'does hell exist?', clearly it is in scripture and nothing in our study so far would, could or should deny this. Nor would I want to argue that hell is not the place of the final punishment of those who reject Jesus as their saviour. On these points, most Christian's agree. The real issue is **what happens to the lost in hell and how long does it happen for?**

Did Jesus teach that *Gehenna* is the place where sinners will suffer eternal torment or the place of the permanent destruction of those who are lost? To find an answer to this question, let's examine what Jesus actually said about hell.

### What Is Hell–*Gehenna?*

Before looking at Jesus's references to *gehenna,* its helpful to look at where this Greek word itself comes from.

Gehenna is the "Valley of Hinnon," located south of Jerusalem. In ancient times, it was linked with the practice of sacrificing children to the god Molech (2 Kings 16:3; 21:6; 23:10). In the days of Hezekiah the valley was used for a huge bonfire for the 185,000 corpses of Assyrian soldiers slain by God (Is 30:31-33; 37:36). The prophet Jeremiah predicted that the place would be called "the valley of slaughter" because it would be filled with the corpses of the Israelites when God judged them for their sins. (Jer 7:32f). Later the Hebrew historian, Josephus tells us that the same valley was heaped with the dead bodies of the Jews following the AD70 siege of Jerusalem.

## Flippin' Hell

Though the imagery of the *gehenna* is common in the Jewish literature, the description of what happens there is contradictory. With this in mind let's look at the 7 time Jesus uses *gehenna* in the Gospels.

In The Sermon on the Mount, Jesus says:

*whoever says, 'You fool!' will be liable to the gehenna of fire. Matt 5:22*

Again, He said

*it is better to pluck out the eye or cut off the hand that causes a person to sin than for the whole body go into gehenna. Matt 5:29f*

And a little later Jesus says, it's better to cut off a foot or a hand or pluck out an eye that causes a person to sin than to "be thrown into eternal fire . . . be thrown into the gehenna of fire" (Matt 18:8f).

The same saying is found in Mark, where Jesus 3 times says that it's better to cut off the offending organ than "to go to gehenna, to the unquenchable fire . . . to be thrown into hell, where their worm does not die, and the fire is not quenched" (Mk 9:44, 46-48)

Jesus chides the Pharisees for crossing sea and land to make a convert and then making him "twice as much a child of *gehenna*" (Matt 23:15).

Finally, he warns the Pharisees that they will not "escape being sentenced to gehenna" (Matt 23:33)

When I began to read these seven occurrences, I fully expected them to settle the debate once and for all. Jesus expected eternal punishment in hell. But I was amazed to find that none of them indicates that hell is a place of unending torment. What is eternal or unquenchable is not the punishment, but the fire.

Just like my findings from my study of the Old Testament this fire is unquenchable in the sense that it totally consumes dead bodies.

The implication is clear. Hell is the place of final punishment, which results in the total destruction of soul and body. The fact that Jesus clearly speaks of God destroying both the soul and body in hell shows that it is the place where sinners are ultimately destroyed and not eternally tormented.

I was shocked by these findings because elsewhere Jesus refers to "eternal fire" and "eternal punishment" in the same passages upon which I based my defence of the traditional view. In Matt 18:8f Jesus repeats what He had said about forfeiting a part of the body in order to escape the "eternal fire" of hell. An even clearer reference to "eternal fire" is found in the parable of the Sheep and the Goats where Jesus speaks of the separation of the saved and the unsaved. He will welcome the faithful into His kingdom, but will reject the wicked, saying: "Depart from me, you cursed, into eternal fire prepared for the devil and his angels; . . . And they will go away into eternal punishment, but the righteous into eternal life" Matt 25:41, 46

By the time I came to study this last passage I had already been shaken by my findings in the Old Testament and the lenses were beginning to fall from my eyes. I saw that there were three things to note here:

**First**, Jesus is just saying that there are two destinies after our death. The nature of each of the destinies isn't discussed in this passage.

**Second**, the fire is 'eternal' and 'unquenchable,' but what is thrown into the fire would be consumed for ever, not tormented for ever.

**Third**, the fire isn't "eternal" because it never goes out, but because it completely consumes the wicked. (More of this when we look at Rev 20). The word for "eternal" is *'aionios'* and it's often used for the permanence of the result rather than the continuation of a process. For example, Jude 7 says that Sodom and

Gomorrah underwent "a punishment of eternal *'aionios'* fire." But the fire that destroyed the 2 cities didn't burn forever, just until it consumed the victims forever.

**Weeping and Gnashing of Teeth.**

Four times in Matt we are told that on the day of judgment "there shall be weeping and gnashing of teeth" (Matt 8:12; 22:13; 24:51; 25:30).

With my presuppositions I had always assumed that this was proof of eternal punishment for the lost. But when I reread the passages I saw that "weeping and gnashing of teeth" occurs in the context of the separation at the final judgment.

So I looked at passages like Zeph 1:14

*"The great day of the LORD is near, near and hastening fast; the sound of the day of the LORD is bitter; the mighty man cries aloud there"*.

And Ps 112:10

*"The wicked man sees it and is angry; he gnashes his teeth and melts away; the desire of the wicked will perish!"*

## Flippin' Hell

Have we missed the the point of how terrible it will be to miss the cut. To know that we could have had it all but now we have missed it.

When I trained as a Navigator in the Royal Air Force, half way through the two year course we had an option to become low level fast jet guys or go for the bigger aircraft like transport or maritime reconnaissance. The choice was a no brainer for me. I wanted to be fast and low, what we called "mud movers". I had done well at both types of flying and fully expected to be streamed low level. The day the results came through I was devastated to find that I had been selected for the high level course whilst guys who had done worse than me went on to low level training. I demanded to see the boss of our unit and was granted an interview. I put on my best uniform and marched into his office, saluted and took a seat. I spent 30 minutes and convinced the Wing Commander that I should be given a chance at the low level course. I was ecstatic. This mattered more to me than anything in my life at that time. 6 months later I failed the low level course and was sent to what I considered to be a back water posting on the old K2 Victor force. It took me a year or more to come to terms with my failure to make the grade. I ground my teeth regularly and was utterly distraught.

Have you never gone for something and not got it? Gnashing and grinding of teeth are what follows that kind of frustration and loss.

Actually it was shortly after this that I became a Christian through the ministry of the Base Chaplain where I served. It was also at that time that I picked up my traditional view of hell and began to defend it with what I thought was the best passage where Jesus talks about hell.

## Luke 16:19-31 Rich man and Lazarus

In this part of Luke's gospel the story of the rich man and Lazarus is the last of 6 episodes in a row where Jesus attacks the Pharisees again and again for their false beliefs and practices. I use the word 'story' because that's what it is. It isn't a parable because it contains no similes or analogies etc.

The first question Jesus asks is "who is the rich man" and the listeners know because 5 verses before, the Pharisees were described as "lovers of money" and as "those who justify yourselves before men".

The Rich man is a Pharisee!

Both men die and according to the Pharisees expectation they enter immediately into the applicable world to come. One to a place of torment and the other to a place of comfort. Everything was as the Pharisees expected except the Pharisee was in the wrong place! The purpose of the story becomes very clear. Salvation wasn't based on rewards for leading a good religious life.

In fact the story has absolutely no claim to be about the actual conditions of heaven or hell, their circumstances are the vehicle for the message. A bit like me using men are from Mars and women from Venus to illustrate a point, but in no way believing that I or my wife beamed down in a space ship! (But now I come to think about it!)

When I began to see that nothing I read about Jesus and hell gave me any proof whatsoever for a doctrine of eternal punishment I was utterly confused. I guess that I should have been celebrating a wonderful discovery in my life but it didn't feel that way. I have so many good friends who defend the traditional view of hell and who I consider to be fellow Bible believing evangelicals. We may well have disagreed on all kinds of biblical interpretations, but this was the first time that I felt that there was a very real risk that I was about about to depart company with them on a major issue of doctrine. What was more, I doubted my own findings. How could we have gone through 2,000 years of Christianity and got it wrong?

For these reasons I sat on what I had found and chewed it over for three years before being nudged by friends to present the research to a group of church leaders a few years ago.

After I finished looking at what Jesus said about hell I checked out what the apostle Paul had written.

## Flippin Paul

The first thing that shocked me was that the word "hell" (*gehenna*) doesn't occur in Paul's letters! But the phrase that Paul does use is his warning about the day of wrath.

*"the day of wrath when God's righteous judgment will be revealed. For he will render to every man according to his works: . . . to those who do not obey the truth, but obey wickedness, there will be wrath and fury. There will be tribulation and distress for every human being who does evil, the Jew first and also the Greek" Rom 2:5-9*

I guess I had always read "wrath, fury, tribulation, distress" as evidence of the conscious, eternal torment.

As a good scholar of the Hebrew bible, Paul most likely had Zephaniah in mind, where the prophet speaks of the Day of the Lord as a *"day of wrath ..... a day of distress and anguish, a day of ruin and devastation, a day of darkness and gloom ..... In the fire of his jealous wrath, all the earth shall be consumed; for a full, yea, sudden end he will make of all the inhabitants of the earth" (Zeph 1:15, 18).*

But Paul never alludes to the everlasting torment of the lost.

Why? Because for him, eternal life is God's gift given to the saved at Christ's coming (1 Cor 15:53f) and not for everyone. He uniquely uses 2 Greek words for humans which are only normally used about God. 'Immortality' - 'athanasia' and 'incorruptibility' - 'aphtharsia'. But he doesn't use them to suggest that they are for humans now, those in Christ get them at the resurrection.

I have to say folks that I was now convinced that I had been wrong about hell. When I went on to look at the other epistles I found nothing to shake my new conviction. But I was very mindful that I hadn't yet got to he real hum dinger. The Book of Revelation.

## CHAPTER SEVEN
## FLIPPIN' REVELATION

Ah, the book of Revelation, surely this must be the place to find some fire and brimstone. This is where Dante got his inspiration. We're sure to find some thing here, aren't we?

Well the two Revelation passages often referred to in support of the idea of everlasting punishment in hell are:

1. The vision of God's Wrath in Rev 14:9-11
2. The vision of the lake of fire and of the 2nd death in Rev 20:10, 14f

Even though I have always known that these passages are highly figurative language, I've found it really hard to let go of the graphic imagery of hell. I guess that a quick google image search on "hell" will show you why. I'll pause whilst you do the search......

Its terrible stuff isn't it? Horrendous pictures of fire and suffering and all manner of evil scenes, there is even a picture of the chef Gordon Ramsey!?

My point is that, if a picture paints a thousand words, we have engrained in our minds that these images must be the real hell. And so we read Revelation through bizarrely distorted lenses. Lets look at the two visions in some detail.

## 1. The Vision of God's Wrath.

In the first of our two passages, John sees three angels announcing God's final judgment. The 3rd angel cries out:

*"If anyone worships the beast and its image and receives a mark on his forehead or on his hand, he also will drink the wine of God's wrath, poured full strength into the cup of his anger, and he will be tormented with fire and sulphur in the presence of the holy angels and in the presence of the Lamb. And the smoke of their torment goes up forever and ever, and they have no rest, day or night, these worshipers of the beast and its image, and whoever receives the mark of its name."*

The angel's loud voice that shouts of God's judgment upon those who worship the beast comes in four parts:

i. The pouring and drinking of the wine of God's wrath.
ii. The torment with fire and sulphur of the ungodly.
iii. The smoke of their torment..
iv. They have no rest day or night.

Lets look at each of the four parts in turn to see what light they throw on our understanding of John's vision.

i. The cup of God's wrath comes straight out of the Old Testament as a symbol of divine judgment (Isa 51:17, 22; Jer 25:15-38; Ps 60:3; 75:8). Here, God pours the full strength cup, so that it is at its most deadly. Later, the same cup is served to Babylon, the city that corrupts the people. God mixes "a double portion for her," and the result is "plagues, death, mourning, and famine" and burned up by fire (Rev 18:6, 8).

Surely the point is that the end of Babylon by fire is also the end of those who drink God's full strength cup.

ii. The fate of the ungodly is described through the imagery of the most terrible judgment that ever fell on earth, the destruction by fire and sulphur of Sodom and Gomorrah.

*"He shall be tormented with fire and sulphur, in the presence of the holy angels and in the presence of the Lamb" Rev 14:10*

This imagery is often used in the Bible to signify complete annihilation (Job 18:15-17; Is 30:33; Ezek 38:22). Isaiah describes the fate of Edom in language that's almost the same as Rev 14:10. He says:

*"And the streams of Edom shall be turned into pitch, and her soil into sulphur; her land shall become burning pitch. Night and day it shall not be quenched; its smoke shall go up forever .."* Isa 34:9f

This of course doesn't mean that Edom will burn forever because the verse continues:

"From generation to generation it shall lie waste; none shall pass through it for ever and ever" Isa 34:10

Obviously these are metaphoric descriptions of destruction, and annihilation.

iii. John, again seeing quite familiar Old Testament images, uses fire and smoke to describe the fate of Babylon. The city "shall be burned up with fire" (Rev 18:8) and "the smoke from her goes up for ever and ever" (Rev 19:3).

Obviously Babylon doesn't burn forever and ever because the kings and merchants cry:

*"Alas, alas, you great city ... In a single hour all this wealth has been laid waste ... and shall be found no more"* Rev 18:10-21

iv. When I used to have no option but to believe in eternal torment the phrase "they have no rest, day or night" (Rev 14:11) seemed to support my traditional view. But need it be the only way to read this verse? John uses the same phrase "day and night" to describe the living creatures praising God (Rev 4:8), the martyrs serving God (Rev 7:15), Satan accusing the brethren (Rev 12:10), and then those being tormented in the lake of fire (Rev 20:10). In each case, the thought is the same: the action continues while it lasts.

In Isa 34:10 Edom's fire is not quenched "night and day" and "its smoke shall go up for ever". The imagery is designed to convey that Edom's fire would last until it had burned up all that there was, and then it would go out. It would be permanent destruction, not everlasting burning.

So, when we read Rev 14:9-11 without our presupposition of eternal torment we can see that the four parts of the judgement complement one another in describing the final destruction of those who worship the beast.

## 2. The vision of the lake of fire and the second death

Possibly the last description in the Bible of the final punishment comes in our second passage and contains two highly significant metaphorical expressions:

## Flippin' Hell

The lake of fire and the second death (Rev 19:20; 20:10, 15; 21:8).

Anyone who has ever seen paintings of the lake of fire has their minds already predisposed to the lake of fire as a synonym for the eternal place of torment. But to see the real meaning of "the lake of fire," we need to put those cruel images to one side and look to the real source of truth. We need to examine the four occurrences of the "lake of fire" found in Revelation, the only book in the Bible where the phrase occurs.

The first reference is found in Rev 19:20, the beast and the false prophet "were thrown alive into the lake of fire that burns with sulphur."

The second reference is found in Rev 20:10,

*"The devil who had deceived them was thrown into the lake of fire and sulphur where the beast and the false prophet were, and they will be tormented day and night for ever and ever."*

The third and fourth references are found in Rev 20:15 and 21:8, where all the wicked are also thrown into the lake of fire.

The million dollar question is whether those who agree with Dante are right and the lake of fire represents an ever-burning hell where the wicked are supposed to be tormented for all eternity, or whether it symbolises the permanent destruction of sin and sinners.

When I took off my Dante glasses I found that five major factors led me to believe that the lake of fire represents the final and complete annihilation of evil and evildoers.

1. The beast and the false prophet are two symbolic figures. Rather than representing actual people they are the persecuting civil governments and the false religion. Governments and religions can't suffer conscious torment forever. So, for them, the lake of fire represents complete annihilation. The end of bad government and false religion.

2. The description of the devil and his host is largely taken from Ezek 38 & 39, where even the names "Gog" and "Magog" are found, and from 2 King 1:10, which tells us about the fire that came down from heaven to consume the officer and the 50 soldiers sent against Elijah. Both times the fire causes the annihilation of evildoers (Ezek 38:22; 39:6, 16).

3. The devil and his angels are spiritual and not physical beings so it's impossible for them to be subjected to real fire, day and night for eternity (Rev 20:10).

4. The fact that "Death and Hades were thrown into the lake of fire" (Rev 20:14) shows that the

meaning of the lake of fire is symbolic, because Death and Hades aren't things that can be thrown into a lake of any kind let alone one of fire! God is revealing to John the complete destruction of death and the grave.

5. The lake of fire is defined as "the second death." It's the complete opposite of "eternal life" that Jesus brings us. In the Bible death is the end of life and not the separation of the body from the soul as in Greek thought.

Now here's an important observation on the way that throughout the book of Revelation, John explains the meaning of the first thing he sees in his vision through the use of a second example. So he explains that the golden bowls of incense which are the prayers of the saints (Rev 5:8). The fine linen is the righteous deeds of the saints (Rev 19:8). The coming to life of the saints and their reigning with Christ for a thousand years is the first resurrection (Rev 20:5).

In the same way, "the lake of fire is the second death" (Rev 20:14). The first death is a temporary sleep because it is followed by the resurrection, and the second death is permanent because there's no end.

Like many of the images in Revelation, the phrase "second death" is found nowhere else in the New Testament but it occurs four times in this last book of the Bible.

The first mention of "second death" is found in Rev 2:11 "The one who conquers will not be hurt by the second death". So the saved gain eternal life, and won't be subjected to eternal death.

We find the second reference in Rev 20:6 "Over such the second death has no power". Again, the newly raised saints won't experience the second death because, hallelujah, we will be raised to eternal life.

In the third and fourth occurrences in Rev 20:14 and 21:8, the 2nd death is identified with the lake of fire into which the devil, the beast, the false prophet, Death, Hades, and all evildoers are thrown. (Crowded enough already!)

Here the lake of fire is the 2nd death because it causes the eternal death and destruction of sin & sinners.

Now I'm sure that some who read this will not be satisfied with my very quick look at just a couple of passages from John's vision of the apocalypse, but I hope that you can see that, if we dare to take away Dante and his fellow hell fire and brimstone creators, we don't have to read the vision in a way which compels us to accept a doctrine which everything else in us rejects.

# CHAPTER EIGHT
# NOW I'M FLIPPIN' CONFUSED

After I'd spent a summer reading everything I could find on what the Bible tells us about judgment, immortality, punishment, heaven and hell etc. I was very confused. Probably about as confused as you are having reached this chapter. I think it was about this time in my studies that the title for this booklet came to mind as I sat at a desk (well more of a picnic table) under a vine in the South of France one morning and muttered to my self "Flippin Hell".

In case you are tempted to exclaim the same as me, let me try and clarify where we have got to so far.

**First**, when years ago I was forced to conclude that the traditional doctrine of hell must be the correct one, I had a niggling thought that the argument didn't start in the right place. In my more recent studies I've found that my unease wasn't unfounded. The traditional view of hell largely depends upon a dualistic view of human nature, which requires us to believe that we are immortal in our own right. The soul will either be in glory or in torment in hell. We've seen that such a belief is foreign to the Biblical view of human nature, where death is more often the end of life for the whole person.

**Second**, although I was happy to accept symbolism in much of the Bible, my view of hell rested largely on a literal interpretation of things like *gehennah,* the lake of fire, and the second death. I hope I have shown that these images don't lend themselves to a literal interpretation because they are metaphorical descriptions of the permanent destruction of the wicked.

**Third**, I started with the niggling thought that the traditional view didn't give me a good explanation for why God would inflict endless divine retribution on someone, for sins committed during the space of a short life. In other words the doctrine of eternal conscious torment is incompatible with the revelation in the rest of scripture of God's wonderful love, mercy, grace and justice.

The traditional view of hell was more likely to be accepted during the Middle Ages, when most people lived under the tyranny of despotic rulers, who could and did torture and destroy human beings much like the inferno which Dante graphically described. Most of us today would regard those regimes as evil and would see a god who inflicted that kind of punishment as evil too. In fact it is scripture itself that has given us our sense of justice which requires that the penalty inflicted must fit the crime.

We began by looking at the three early church opinions on the fate of the wicked: Irenaeus, Gregory of Nyssa, and Augustine.

We might call those views conditional immortality, universalism, and unending punishment, respectively.

When we looked at the Old Testament evidence we found that the early Israelites had little expectation of life after death but by the last few centuries before Christ they were beginning to think about a continuation of life after death for the people of God.

The early period between the two halves of the Bible continued to develop these thoughts and the idea of a place to go to after death was explored.

In the New Testament we found that under the Pharisees the dominant thought was that there would be a place where the good Jews would go to be with God. We looked at the story of the rich man and Lazarus as a typical example of Jesus using their expectations to make a point about their self-centredness.

The fate of the unrighteous wasn't as clear but it looks like a loss of life or consignment to death/destruction was envisaged.

It is fair to say that there are 2 major passages (Jn 5:29 & Rev 20:11-15) and a few other indications of the expectation of a resurrection for judgement of the wicked for the purpose of condemnation.

It is very clear that there is no evidence that the unrighteous will be made righteous and restored.

All of this means that:

The New Testament will not allow the subject of hell to be side lined or dismissed just because it feels wrong. The subject of eternal life, or not, is consistently addressed because salvation begs the question 'what happens to the lost?'

# CHAPTER NINE
# TWO OTHER FLIPPIN' DAFT IDEAS

Our story of Sgt Jones caused us to ask "would God do that to my friends and family if they didn't confess Jesus as their saviour?" Lots of people have asked the same question and as we saw earlier, some have come up with positions which are anything but new. But the question nonetheless remains, are there biblically viable answers?

Lets look at the other two popular answers given as alternatives to eternal torment in hell.

The first is the metaphorical view, which regards hell as a place where the suffering is more mental than physical. The fire isn't literal but metaphorical, and the pain is caused more by the sense of separation from God than by any physical torment from lakes of fire. The second alternative is the universalist view of hell, which turns hell into a purging, refining fire that ultimately makes it possible for everybody to make it into heaven. I'll try to give a quick overview of both positions.

## 1. The Metaphorical View of Hell

The least controversial alternative to the traditional view of hell involves interpreting metaphorically the nature of the unending torment of hell.

According to this view, hell is still understood as everlasting punishment, but not physical torture, because the fire no longer burns the victims, but represents the pain of being separated from God. A bit like saying my heart burned with passion for my wife.

At first glance the metaphorical view seems very attractive. Those who hold the view rightly point out that the images used in the Bible to describe hell, like fire, darkness, voracious maggots, sulphur, and gnashing of teeth are metaphors and not actual descriptions of fact.

Metaphors are designed to communicate a particular message, but they're not the message, just the vehicle to get the point across.

I might say 'I was broken hearted when West Bromwich Albion got knocked out of the FA Cup, I was completely crushed at the way we defended and missing the penalty in extra time killed me'. Clearly my chosen vehicle of broken, crushed and killed was violent to say the least but it wasn't the real message.

Those who hold the metaphorical view are correct in pointing out that the big problem with the traditional view of hell is that it's based on a literalism that ignores the hugely symbolic nature of the language used. But the problem is that they just want to replace the physical torment with a supposedly more humane mental torment. But lowering the physical pain level in a non-literal hell, doesn't really change it's nature, because it's still a place of unending torment. Not 26 years, or a hundred years or a million years, but never ending. That kind of mental torture is surely as wrong as physical pain. Sgt Jones was able to be physically patched up, but mentally he could never recover.

So turning the temperature down in hell isn't the answer to our problem. We need to understand the nature of the final punishment which, as we have seen, is permanent annihilation and not eternal torment.

## 2. The Universalist View of Hell

Those who hold to a universalists view of hell believe that God will eventually bring every human being to salvation and eternal life. No one will be condemned in the final judgment to either eternal torment or annihilation, although variations on this theme see the wicked as being required to spend some time in a place where they can learn the error of their ways. (Not unlike the old Roman Catholic notion of purgatory).

Although first suggested by Origen in the third century, this view has gained steady support in modern times, especially through the writing of men like Friedrich Schleiermacher, C.F.D. Moule, J.A.T. Robinson, W H Vanstone, and John Hick. Most recently the popular writing of Rob Bell and Brian McClaren have strongly hinted at this alternative to eternal damnation and punishment and have presented both theological and philosophical ideas in support of universalism.

## Theological and Philosophical Arguments.

There is a common list of scriptures (1 Tim 2:4; 4:10; Col 1:20; Rom 5:18; 11:32; Eph 1:10; 1 Cor 15:22), which seem to hint that all will eventually be saved. For instance, a universalist might say: 'It's God's will for "all men to be saved and to come to the knowledge of the truth" (1 Tim 2:4).

I tend to agree with universalists on their philosophical position. They find it intolerable that a loving God would allow millions of people to suffer everlasting torment for sins committed within a span of a few (sometime tragically few) years. But many of the recent popular writing from those who also agree with this philosophical argument are very unhelpful in presenting the theological position and leave the reader with lots of questions which undermine the traditional view without giving enough help to come to a truly biblical response. Readers can be left with thoughts that the universalist position must be true purely on a good philosophical argument. You have most likely had questions from friends along the lines of:

**'Would God really condemn millions of non-Christians who haven't responded to Christ because they have never heard the gospel?'**

It would be great if we could answer that 'God will save all the unfaithful by enabling them to be gradually transformed through a purifying process after death. Beyond death, God continues to draw all the unsaved to Himself, until ultimately they will all respond to His love and rejoice in His presence for all eternity.' However, we cant say that because, as appealing as it might be, it's a wholly unbiblical view.

Anyone who has been affected by God's love, wants to see Him saving everyone. I hate to think that He would be so vindictive as to eternally torture millions of people - especially those who have lived in ignorance. Or those who have been put off by the appalling lack of love from churches. But, whilst I really appreciate the provocation of men like Rob Bell in 'Love wins' and I defend the universalists' concern to uphold the triumph of God's love and to counter the unbiblical concept of eternal suffering. However, I can't come to any other opinion on universalism than it is a serious distortion of Biblical teaching.

When, at college I faced my first crisis with the doctrine of hell I was reminded that the universalist tend to take the key passages of the Bible out of context.

For instance Col 1:20 God's plan "to reconcile to himself all things" is actually set in the context of Col 1:19-23 It is said to the Colossian believers, "provided that you continue in the faith." Another example often used is 1 Tim 2:4, God's desire is for "all men to be saved". But this comes with the fact of a final judgment that will bring "ruin and destruction" to the unfaithful (1 Tim 6:9f).

God's offer of salvation is to everyone, but He respects the freedom of those who reject His offer even though it causes Him immeasurable pain.

## Universal salvation can't be right just because eternal suffering is wrong.

The notion of punishment for a time to bring about true repentance, or of gradual transformation after death, is totally foreign to the Scripture.

The destiny of each person is firmly fixed at death. Hence Heb 9:27

> *"it is appointed for men to die once, and after that comes judgment."*

Of course there is always the question about those who had no opportunity to respond to the message of Christ because of life circumstances. "What will happen to the tribesman who never heard the gospel?" But the Bible gives us good grounds not to worry that they will be condemned purely on this single fact. Paul mentions that the gentiles who don't know the law will be judged according to the law which is "written in their hearts" (Rom 2:14-16).

Universalism, though in some ways attractive, is wrong because it fails to recognise that God's love for us isn't demonstrated by ignoring our sins, nor by changing us (with our consent or against our will) after death, but rather by providing salvation and freedom to accept it.

**For God so loved the world that he gave his only Son, that whoever believes in him should not perish but have eternal life (Jn 3:16)**

Both the metaphorical and universalistic views of hell are attempts at "flippin hell". But honestly, when I read some of the popular books which are around today they are much more likely to cause me to cry "Flippin Hell!"

The only biblical solution to the problems of the traditionalist view isn't found through lowering the temperature of hell but, by accepting hell for what it is, the terrible and final punishment and permanent annihilation of the wicked.

**"The wicked will be no more"** Ps 37:10

**"their end is destruction"** Phil 3:19

## CHAPTER TEN
## SO WHAT THE FLIPPIN' HELL DOES IT LOOK LIKE IN HELL?

When I began to change my views on hell as a place of eternal torment I became quite fearful that I was slipping into a heresy. It seemed as though I was possibly playing into Satan's trap and there would be no way back. One of the reasons this fear came in was because the annihilation view of hell has been associated mostly with "sects" like the Seventh-day Adventists, Jehovah's Witnesses, and some Sabbatarian churches. In fact many evangelicals and Roman Catholics have rejected annihilation, simply because it's a belief held by many cults and not a traditional Protestant or Catholic stance.

As I finish writing this book it is 6 weeks before the 500th anniversary of Martin Luther purportedly nailing his thesis to the church door at Wittenberg and thus beginning the Reformation.

One thing the reformation taught us was that we can't just rely on tradition. As Christians, we can't afford to become enslaved to any human tradition, whether it be "Catholic" tradition, "Evangelical" tradition, or even our own denomination's claims. John Stott wrote:

## Flippin' Hell

*"I am hesitant to have written these things, partly because I have great respect for long-standing tradition which claims to be a true interpretation of Scripture, and do not lightly set it aside, and partly because the unity of the worldwide evangelical community has always meant much to me. But the issue is too important to be suppressed, and I am grateful to you [David Edwards] for challenging me to declare my present mind. I do not dogmatise about the position to which I have come. I hold it tentatively. But I do plead for frank dialogue among evangelicals on the basis of Scripture."*

Emotional and Biblical reasons caused John Stott to abandon the traditional view of hell and adopt the annihilation view. He goes on,

*"Emotionally, I find the concept (of eternal torment) intolerable and do not understand how people can live with it without either cauterising their feelings or cracking under the strain. But our emotions are a fluctuating, unreliable guide to truth and must not be exalted to the place of supreme authority in determining it. As a committed Evangelical, my question must be - and is - not what my heart tells me, but what does God's word say? And in order to answer this question, we need to survey the Biblical material afresh and to open our minds (not just our hearts) to the possibility that Scripture points in the direction of annihilationism, and that 'eternal conscious*

*torment' is a tradition which has to yield to the supreme authority of Scripture."*

In response to Stott's plea to take a fresh look at the Biblical teaching on the final punishment, let's look at the Scriptures through our new lenses.

The Old and New Testaments seem to agree:

*"The soul who sins shall die" Ezek 18:4, 20*

*"The wages of sin is death" Rom 6:23*

Right at the outset we can see that the ultimate wages of sin is not eternal torment, but permanent death. For Christians death as we know it, would indeed be the end of our existence were it not for the fact of the resurrection (1 Cor 15:18). It's the resurrection that turns death into a sleep and then removes its sting completely as we rise to eternal life. But as we saw earlier, there's no resurrection from the second death. It is the end of life.

In the Old Testament sacrificial system, the penalty for the worst sin was always the death of the substitute sacrifice and never a prolonged torture, rehabilitation, or imprisonment of the victim. The separation that occurred on the Day of Atonement between genuine and false Israelites was a foreshadowing of the separation that will occur at the Second coming. Jesus compared this to harvest time and the separation of the wheat and the tares. The tares were sown among the wheat, which represents "the sons of the kingdom" (Matt 13:38). Wheat and tares, genuine and false believers, will coexist in the church until His coming. On that day of judgement, the real separation foreshadowed by the Day of Atonement will occur.

**Jesus' Death and the Punishment of Sinners.**

Jesus' death on the cross shows us many things but one of these is how God will finally deal with sin and sinners. It's the revelation of the wrath of God against all human ungodliness and unrighteousness (Rom 1:18; cf. 2 Cor 5:21; Mk 15:34). What Jesus experienced on the cross wasn't just the physical death we will all face, but the death that sinners will experience at the final judgment. This is why He was "greatly distressed, troubled . . . very sorrowful, even to death" Mk 14:33f It's no wonder that Jesus felt forsaken by the Father, because He experienced the death that awaits sinners at the final judgment.

If Jesus hadn't been raised, He, and all those who have fallen asleep in Him, would simply have perished (1 Cor 15:18). But they would not have experienced unending torment in hell.

Jesus' resurrection reassures us that those who believe in Him need not fear death, because Christ's death marked the death of death (2 Tim 1:10; Heb 2:14; Rev 20:14). Now I hear the hallelujahs!

## The Language of Destruction in the Bible

After I had taken the summer to study hell and come to a mind that I needed to reconsider my Dante inspired view, I found that there is a huge amount of destruction language used in the Bible to describe the fate of the wicked.

According to experts, 28 Hebrew nouns and 23 verbs are usually translated "destruction" or "to destroy" in our Bibles. And around **half** of these words describe the final destruction of the wicked!

For instance, several Psalms describe the final destruction of the wicked with dramatic imagery (Ps 1:3-6; 2:9-12; 11:1-7; 34:8-22; 58:6-10; 69:22-28; 145:17, 20).

An example would be Psalm 37, the wicked "will soon fade like grass", "they shall be cut off . . . and will be no more", they will "perish . . . like smoke they vanish away", "transgressors shall be altogether destroyed".

The prophets too frequently announce the ultimate destruction of the wicked as part of their visions of the Day of the Lord.

In his opening chapter, Isaiah proclaims that "rebels and sinners shall be destroyed together, and those who forsake the Lord shall be consumed" (Is 1:28). Hosea, uses a variety of images to describe the final end of sinners.

*"They shall be like the morning mist or like the dew that goes early away, like the chaff that swirls from the threshing floor or like smoke from a window" Hos 13:3*

The comparison of the fate of the wicked with the morning mist, the early dew, the chaff, and the smoke hardly suggests that sinners will suffer forever.

Even on the very last page of the Old Testament we find images of the final destiny of believers and unbelievers. For those who fear the Lord, "the sun of righteousness shall rise, with healing in its wings" (Mal 4:2). But for unbelievers the Day of the Lord "comes, burning like an oven, when all the arrogant and all the evildoers will be stubble; the day that comes shall burn them up, says the Lord of host, so that it will leave them neither root nor branch" (Mal 4:1). The day of the final punishment of the lost will also be a day of vindication of God's people, they shall tread down the wicked, for they will be ashes under the soles of [their] feet, on the day when I act, says the Lord of hosts. Mal 4:3.

The Old Testament revelation of the fate of the wicked is total and permanent destruction and not eternal torment.

When I finished my survey of the word "Destruction" in the New Testament my findings were amazingly similar. The most common Greek words are the verb *apollumi* (to destroy) and the noun *apoleia* (destruction). And yet again these are used in very graphic imagery to show the annihilation of the wicked on the last day.

Jesus uses lots of images from nature to illustrate the destruction of the lost. He compares it to:

weeds that are bound in bundles to be burned (Matt 13:30, 40)
bad fish that is *thrown away* (Matt 13:48)
harmful plants that are rooted up (Matt 15:13)
fruitless trees that are cut down (Luke 13:7)
withered branches that are burned (Jn 15:6)

He also used illustrations from human life to show the fate of the wicked:

unfaithful tenants who are destroyed (Lk 20:16)
an evil servant who will be cut in pieces (Matt 24:51)
the Galileans who perished (Lk 13:2f)
the eighteen people crushed by Siloam's tower (Lk 13:4f)
those to be destroyed by the flood (Lk 17:27)
the people of Sodom and Gomorrah destroyed by fire and sulphur(Lk 17:29)
rebellious servants who were slaughtered at the return of their master (Lk 19:27)

The images used by Jesus clearly depict the ultimate destruction of the wicked, but he also taught their fate through very damning pronouncements.

For example, He said:

*"Do not fear those who can kill the body but cannot kill the soul; rather fear him who can destroy both soul and body in hell"*
*Matt 10:28*

John Stott rightly says:

*"If to kill is to deprive the body of life, hell would seem to be the deprivation of both physical and spiritual life, that is, an extinction of being."*

Often Jesus contrasted eternal life with death or destruction.

*"I give them eternal life, and they shall never perish" Jn 10:28*

*"Enter by the narrow gate; for the gate is wide and the way is easy that leads to destruction, and those who enter it are many. For the gate is narrow and the way is hard that leads to life, and those who find it are few" Matt 7:13-14*

Once we have removed our Dante lenses, I can't find any good reason for making the words "perish" or "destruction" mean everlasting torment.

Earlier I pointed out that Jesus used the imagery of Ghent to describe the destruction of the wicked in hell. None of the 7 occurrences indicates that hell is a place of unending torment. What is eternal or unquenchable isn't the punishment but the fire which causes the complete and permanent destruction of the wicked, that lasts forever.

The Apostle Paul doesn't contradict Jesus. When he writes of the "enemies of the cross of Christ," Paul says that "their end is destruction" (Phil 3:19). We could also see the same understanding Gal 6:8, 1 Thess 5:2f, and 2 Thess 1:9. But Rom 2:6-12, is where Paul provides one of the clearest descriptions of the final destiny of believers and unbelievers. God "will render to every man according to his works" (Rom 2:6)... to those who by patience in well-doing seek for glory and honour and immortality, he will give eternal life; but for those who are self-seeking and do not obey the truth, but obey unrighteousness, there will be wrath and fury. There will be tribulation and distress for every human being who does evil, the Jew first and also the Greek (Rom 2:7-9). The wicked don't receive immortality, but "wrath and fury," two words associated with the final judgment (1 Thes 1:10; Rev 14:10; 16:19; 19:15).

Eternal life is God's gift to the saved, but corruption, destruction, death, and perishing are expected for unrepentant sinners.

I could go on to show how Peter and the other New Testament authors should be read in a similar way, but the arguments are quite technical and I hope that I have proved my point several times already.

# CHAPTER ELEVEN
# FLIPPIN' TWO FACED GOD

If I'm being completely honest, my difficulty with the traditional view of hell didn't begin with a biblical argument but with a moral one which started with a question, "How can this view of God as a torturer of the lost be reconciled with the loving God revealed to us in Jesus?"

How can I tell people that God so loved the world that He holds them eternally responsible for their sin in such a way that they will face horrendous fires and agony unless they choose Jesus?

**Does God have two faces?**

Is God wonderfully merciful on one side and insatiably cruel on the other?

Like the head of Janus (above) from Roman mythology.

The next time that you are lost in worship, hands held high, adoring God, ask yourself,

**"Can I really praise God for His goodness, if He torments the lost for eternity?"**

Now I'm very mindful here of Rom 9:20 'But who are you, O man, to answer back to God? Will what is moulded say to its moulder, "Why have you made me like this?"'

We do need to be very careful that we aren't criticising God. But he has given us a mind to enable us to make moral judgments. In fact we are called to treat our fellow man with great love and respect. Nevertheless, over the 2,000 years of Christianity man has done some terrible things in the name of Christ.

Perhaps things would have been very different had we not held the traditional view of hell. After all, if God, who is perfect, can punish those who deny Christ, maybe the church can too. What inspired popes, bishops, church councils, monks, Christian kings and leaders to torture and slaughter their fellow Christians? What influenced, Calvin and the leaders of

Geneva to burn Servetus at the stake for voicing doubt about the Trinity? Perhaps the doctrine of hellfire has been instrumental in justifying religious intolerance, torture, and the killing of heretics.

Of course over the centuries theologians have continually wrestled with the problem of hell and there have been various attempts to turn it's temperature down a degree or two, or at least reduce the numbers of it's inmates. Augustine invented purgatory to reduce the population of hell. Some Christian thinkers have amended the doctrine by allowing for the automatic salvation of children who die in infancy. Still others have changed the doctrine in one way or another to exempt various groups of people from eternal fire. The idea seems to be that, if the total number of those who are going to be tormented is relatively small, there's no reason to be unduly concerned!

Well it leaves me very concerned that people are left with the same problem with God's character. It makes Him no less of a despot. Sgt Jones was just one man but his torture was still immoral and repulsive. Whether God inflicted unending torment on one million or on ten billion sinners, the fact would remain that He torments people everlastingly.

Ultimately, any doctrine of hell should pass the test of moral acceptability, and the traditional doctrine of unending torment doesn't seem to pass such a test. Annihilationism, on the other hand, passes the test for 2 reasons.

First, it doesn't view hell as everlasting torture but as permanent extinction of the wicked.

Second, it recognises that God respects the freedom of those who choose not to be saved. He is morally justified in destroying the wicked because He respects their choice.

People need to learn the fear of God, and this is one reason for preaching on the final judgment and punishment. We need to warn people that those who reject Christ and His death on the cross for their salvation, will ultimately experience judgment and "suffer the punishment of eternal destruction" (2 Thess 1:9).

The annihilation view of the final punishment helps us. We can proclaim the great alternative between eternal life and permanent destruction without fear of portraying God as a monster.

# CHAPTER TWELVE
# FLIPPIN' HELL

I love good news. As I have been writing this last couple of chapters I have heard that one of my nephew's wife has just safely delivered their third child. That's our 11th great nephew or niece. Very good news indeed. Its very peculiar that we call the story of Jesus good news when actually according to traditional belief on hell, for the majority of people its very, very bad news!

People today aren't scared of asking difficult questions and they don't avoid rejecting the answers that they think are totally preposterous.

I recently heard of a lecturer who said that we (the church) must not shy away from proclaiming the traditional view of hell as a place of eternal punishment for the wicked because if we were to do so, we would have nothing with which to drive the wicked to Christ!!! Flippin Hell.

Can you imagine having the winning lottery ticket in your hand and thinking, I'm not sure claiming the 21 million pounds is a good idea? Maybe a friend would try to convince you to claim the prize money. What might they say to you to persuade you? It would undoubtedly be, "Just think of what you can buy, the new house, car, boat, clothes. Imagine the holidays the

## Flippin' Hell

help you could be to family and friends, the opportunity to enjoy life". There's no way the friend would try to convince you by saying "poverty is dreadful, someone else will get the money, do you know how much inflation is going to be this year, you may lose your job next week". No advertising for the National Lottery focusses on the poverty of life. No one buys a lottery ticket thinking about how bad life might be, but how good it could be.

So how come evangelists have spent years telling people about the fires of hell in order to chase them fearfully towards Jesus? Perhaps they don't know how good Jesus really is! Maybe they don't realise how brilliant the Kingdom of God is and how wonderful eternity with Jesus is going to be. I once heard of a Victorian preacher who threw the chapel cat into the heating furnace to demonstrate to the Sunday School children how terrible hell will be! I'm told that the cat did a great impression of a dog as it went "woof". Sorry cat lovers!

If we feel that we have to concentrate on a negative to drive people to Jesus, perhaps we haven't grasped how awesome our God really is, how amazing His grace and how beautiful his nature. Why on earth would I want to refuse eternity in His presence where thing get better and better. As C S Lewis puts it in his Narnia series book "The Last Battle" as the children go into eternity:

*"But for them it was only the beginning of the real story. All their life in this world and all their adventures in Narnia had only been the cover and the title page: now at last they were beginning Chapter One of the Great Story which no one on earth has read: which goes on for ever: in which every chapter is better than the one before."*

I used to worry about annihilation because I thought that it was cheap justice to allow those who reject Jesus to 'just die'. My thoughts went along the lines of, "Its not fair, they could sin in all kinds of ways and reject the gospel and they will get away with it. No punishment. While I have to be good and watch them enjoy life! People will carry on sinning because they will be happy with being dead for eternity"

There was so much wrong with my old thinking:

1. Sin isn't good in any way shape or form. They are missing out on the relationship with Jesus right now. And that relationship is the best thing on earth bar none.

2. Its not fair that any one, let alone me, should receive eternal life when I too deserve death.

3. "They" aren't getting way with anything. They will be judged and found wanting and

despatched to hell where they will be consumed forever.

4. Why would I be jealous of people who are in darkness when I am in the light?

5. Its not just death for the lost. Death is the opposite of life in all its fulness (Jn 10:10) for eternity. You don't need to be conscious of your punishment to receive it. Contrary to Captain Hook's view to die would not be "a great adventure" to live forever in God's Kingdom will be.

6. If someone is left thinking that death is a better option than eternity with God, we have badly represented Jesus and His kingdom.

We have to learn to re think on hell. To Flip our thinking once and for all. But not just on hell, on heaven and the new earth and God's Kingdom too.

If our Christian living and our future hope doesn't cause people to rush to Jesus like crowds on the first morning of the January sales in Oxford street then we have to flippin' change.

Jesus said I am the good shepherd. I know my own and my own know me.... My sheep hear my voice, and I know them, and they follow me. (John 10:14,27)

People follow Jesus, they hear His voice and follow. Paul said it was like following a wonderful fragrance (2 Cor :14). We're more inclined to tell people to come away from the stink of the sewer! Flippin' hell.

Dare we be real about grace, love and mercy whilst remaining truly biblical. Dare we take off our Dante issue glasses. Dare we risk the taunt of those who are yet to take off their glasses who will think we have become heretics like Jehovah Witnesses or Mormons. Or dare we continue to paint a picture of our wonderful God as having two faces with a hidden horrible nature who condemns and punishes people for eternity for their sins committed in a very short life time?

The doctrine of hell is by no means the most important one in Scripture, but it certainly affects the way we understand what the Bible teaches in other vital areas such as human nature, death, salvation, God's character, human destiny, and the world to come. The traditional view of hell is either right or wrong and its either right or wrong because of what the Bible teaches us and no other reason. We have looked for evidence to support a doctrine of eternal punishment by fire and have found no remaining Biblical support for it.

## Flippin' Hell

Today the traditional view of hell is being challenged and abandoned by respected scholars of different denominational persuasions, for all kinds of reasons. Maybe they were good reasons to begin the journey to find a truly biblical view. But the only acceptable answer to the dilemma of hell is to look to the rich imagery and language of destruction used throughout the Bible to portray the fate of the lost which clearly indicates that their final punishment results in annihilation and not eternal, conscious torment.

The objections to such a view are so strong and the support so weak that more and more people are abandoning it, and adopting instead the notion of universal salvation in order to avoid the sadistic horror of hell. To salvage the important Biblical doctrine of the final judgment and punishment of the wicked, it's important for Bible believing Christians to reexamine what the Bible really teaches about the fate of the lost.

Our careful investigation of the relevant Biblical data has shown that the wicked will be resurrected for the purpose of divine judgment. This day of judgement will involve a permanent expulsion from God's presence into a place where there will be weeping and grinding of teeth. After God's justice has been pronounced, the wicked will be consumed with no hope of restoration or recovery. The ultimate restoration of believers and the extinction of sinners from this world will prove that Christ's redemptive mission has been an unqualified victory.

Christ's victory means that "the former things have passed away" (Rev 21:4), and that only His light, love, peace, and joy will continue for all eternity. And those in Christ shall reign with Him. Hallelujah!

I am aware that other wiser and more knowledgeable Christians have said all that I have written here and more. They were pioneers of the view I have come to. However, they were not well received by the evangelical church today. Some were hounded out of their ministries by fearful Christians who felt that to deny the traditional view of hell would be the slippery slope into liberal thinking, heresy and a loss of faith. I have great sympathy with both parties. After all they are my brothers and sisters whom I look forward to eternity with.

I have not slammed the lid on all further debate on the issues discussed in this book. I welcome biblical scholars to correct me and enlighten me. The debate continues. I only ask that we make it a truly biblical debate.

I am about to leave Church leadership after 30 years or more. My wife and I are establishing a residential centre where others can come and rest, pray and share together over meals and fellowship. I welcome you to come and stay with us and in love and mutual respect continue this and many other debates. Let's wrestle with scripture together.

# BIBLIOGRAPHY

**Four Views on Hell**
by William Crockett (Editor), Stanley N. Gundry (Series Editor), John F. Walvoord, Zachary J. Hayes, Clark H. Pinnock

**Four Views on Hell**
Second Edition (Counterpoints: Bible and Theology) by Preston Sprinkle (Editor), Denny Burk, John G. Stackhouse Jr., Robin Parry, Jerry Walls

**Hell on trial: The case for eternal punishment**
Robert Peterson

**The Fire That Consumes: A Biblical and Historical Study of the Doctrine of the Final Punishment**
Edward Fudge

**The Book of Revelation (The New International Commentary on the New Testament)**
Robert Mounce

**The doctrine of eternal punishment**
Harry Buis

**'Hell': A Hard Look at a Hard Question: The Fate of the Unrighteous in New Testament Thought**
David Powys

**Issue facing Christians Today**
John Stott

**The Relevance of John's Apocalypse**
Donald Guthrie

**A commentary on Daniel**
Andre Lecoque

Printed in Great Britain
by Amazon